ARKANSAS: YEAR OF AMERICAN CRAFT 1993

The Arkansas Arts Center Decorative Arts Museum
The Pike-Fletcher-Terry House
July 4 - August 15, 1993

The Arkansas Arts Center Decorative Arts Museum
The Pike-Fletcher-Terry House

East Seventh and Rock Streets
P.O. Box 2137
Little Rock, Arkansas 72203-2137

Telephone: 501-372-4000
Fax: 501-375-8053

Director and Chief Curator: Townsend Wolfe
Curator of Decorative Arts: Alan DuBois
Curatorial Assistant: Karen Bryant

Photography: Pg. No. 25 by Cindy Momchilov, Pg. No. 27 courtesy of the artist, all others by Bill Parsons

Editorial Note: All dimensions are given in inches; height precedes width. Use of this symbol "■" denotes work illustrated.

Copyright © 1993 The Arkansas Arts Center

Printed in the U.S.A.
by Little Rock Printing
Little Rock, Arkansas

This catalogue has been underwritten by an anonymous donor to whom the museum and craftspersons of Arkansas express deep appreciation.

Season Sponsors: Beverly Enterprises, Inc., Giroir & Gregory, P.A., Ernst & Young, Leisure Arts, Inc.

This project is supported in part by the Arkansas Arts Council.

Contents

Introduction   6

Catalogue

Gayle Batson	8
David Blaisus & Jeanmarie Rain Mako	10
Joe Bruhin	12
Nancy Jane Collins	14
James Cottey	16
David & Becky Dahlstedt	18
Stephen Driver	20
Michael Haley & Susy Siegele	22
Thom Hall	24
Irma Gail Hatcher	26
Sharon Heidingsfelder	28
Robyn Horn	30
Kaye Martinez	32
Shep Miers	34
Mary Morgan	36
John Mori	38
Keith Newton	40
Leon & Sharon Niehues	42
Ed & Amy Pennebaker	44
Helen Phillips	46
Laura Phillips	48
Liz Powers	50
Owen Rein	52
Douglas Stowe	54
Mark Werner	56

Biographies   58

Introduction

This catalogue documents an exhibition that is a part of the 1993 Year of American Craft celebration throughout the Western Hemisphere. The museum's focus is contemporary American crafts and its goal is to bring artists and their work before an understanding and appreciative public, so it seems ideal for us to recognize Arkansas's finest craftspersons not only with an exhibition, but also with a full-color catalogue. This will serve as a benchmark for craft objects and become a tool for promoting craftspersons in this state. We hope other states will do the same.

In selecting these 25 artists, the museum staff drew upon artists represented in its permanent collection, winners of its competitive Regional Craft Biennial exhibition, members of The Arkansas Craft Guild and applicants to the Arkansas Arts Council's visual artists fellowship awards for 1993. All of the artists were visited in their studios and were photographed and interviewed on tape between September 1992 and May 1993.

The interviews can only be summarized. Many artists are native Arkansans, but equally impressive are those who moved to the state as part of the back to the land and counterculture movements of the late 1960s and 1970s. Many sought out Northwest Arkansas where an Ozark craft tradition existed, land was cheap, laws unrestricting, natural materials plentiful and social, cultural and aesthetic barriers were falling rapidly. All came with the notion of making a living with their hands. Twenty to 30 years later the ranks have thinned. Only the strong hearted prevail. We salute their courage.

Today's work varies as much as the artists and their markets. While all the objects incorporate craft media - clay, fiber, glass, metal and wood - some are plainly functional; others address aesthetics frequently associated with painting or sculpture. Likewise expression varies from naive to elegantly sophisticated. Their work habits may go from the one-person craft studio turning out 10 one-of-a-kind pieces a year and selling only to a local market with gross sales of $3,000 annually to a five-person studio producing thousands of original works and selling wholesale to a national market with gross sales of $110,000.

Arkansas has a rich legacy in these artists that should be nurtured and encouraged. Their deeply rooted presence in the state, their tenacity, desire to understand their mediums and instill works with new energy can only serve to enrich our lives and provide a source of pride for our state and nation. ADB

Gayle Batson

A native Arkansan, Batson fondly remembers summers and holidays on Uncle Pink's hilltop farm in the Ozark Mountains and making leaf forms out of clay. She always was interested in music and the visual arts but it was not until her junior year in college that the artist decided on her life goal to work in clay. After marriage, and a few years in Tulsa, Oklahoma, Batson returned to Little Rock and continued to take classes and teach at The Arkansas Arts Center. A dance exercise class helped her with throwing on the wheel, which she finds relaxing.

She first made functional pottery, gradually adding "little beasties" to her pots. Next came a series of "creepy crawly finger spiders." In 1981-1982 she began sawdust firing; she has a general idea of what the chemicals and smoke will do, but likes giving up control of the outcome. Her forms are soft and reflect an interest in nature, especially mushrooms, bones and river washed stones. She has adopted the practice of sealing up her forms with things that will rattle and secret messages. "The inside of the pot is mysterious and still mine," she states. The stone and bone gardens, which the viewer can arrange, began in the early 1980s and are reminders of prehistoric sites. A gregarious extrovert, she presents the other side of herself - quiet, contemplative - in her pottery.

1. ***Sticks & Stones***, 1992
   sawdust-fired porcelain & stoneware, acrylic paint
   5 1/2 x 14 1/2 diameter

2. ***Kernos***, 1992
   stoneware, copper carbonate & pink stain, straw wrapped then sawdust-fired
   17 1/2 x 16 1/2 diameter

David Blaisus & Jeanmarie Rain Mako

Blaisus and Mako are from Minnesota. They had politically active parents and read avidly about pioneers as children. Blaisus is 16 hours short of his college degree. Mako studied anthropology and early childhood education, which included an internship in a one room school house in Ireland. They moved to Arkansas at the invitation of friends and had a vague notion of making a living from crafts. They reasoned they didn't need much money and they could live in the wilderness close to nature. Running out of money they took a basket making workshop and produced their first baskets in 1984. Both struggled with a temperament for perfection and nearly had a "complete falling out." They learned quickly however, that people invariably sought their best work and that they were capable of producing something finer than the traditional Arkansas work basket.

In a good year they will make 100 to 200 baskets. Having two children has slowed their basket making somewhat but has also helped them sharpen their skills. "The idea of making a basket," Blaisus explained, "is to show the quality of the wood." In the past three years they have experimented with twill and diamond-shape patterns. Their works are functional, decorative and full of integrity. "Basket making plays on all our talents and has been a real stretching experience," said Blaisus.

■ 3. *Picnic Basket*, 1993
   white oak
   7 1/2 x 16 x 11

4. *Round Basket with Twill Woven Pattern*, 1993
   white oak,
   15 x 10 1/2 x 11

Joe Bruhin

At age 15 Bruhin began hitchhiking and backpacking in Colorado, California and Washington and after high school traveled to Florida, the East Coast and Canada. These experiences taught him to be independent, get by on very little, and to realize that he would live in the country one day. He enlisted in the Army so he and his young bride could travel abroad. Upon his discharge in Europe they traveled with their son around Europe, Africa and Asia.

He was introduced to clay by a friend at junior college. One and a half years later, at Sun Valley Ranch, Utah, he learned wood firing and met people who had a passion for clay. Returning to St. Louis in 1983 he began looking for 40 acres with plenty of water, which he eventually found near Fox, Arkansas. By living in a tepee and planting trees to earn money for three winters, the Bruhins were able to move into the cabin they built. His wood-firing kiln was built next and recently, with the aid of a fellowship from the Arkansas Arts Council, he completed a separate studio. Bruhin describes working in the studio "as almost holy... it is the closest thing I have to church." Throwing for him is a dance in which "I let it happen," he says. He speaks of his pieces being invested with an energy that comes from his physical involvement, the wood fire and something outside of him.

5. *Bowl*, 1993
   stoneware, orange slip, wood-fired
   4 1/2 x 15 3/4 diameter

6. *Faceted Cup*, 1993
   porcelain, unglazed, wood-fired
   4 1/2 x 3 1/2 x 3 1/4 diameter

7. *Covered Jar*, 1993
   porcelaineous stoneware, wood-fired
   8 x 9 3/4 diameter

■ 8. *Covered Jar*, 1993
   stoneware, wood-fired
   12 x 12 3/4 diameter

Nancy Jane Collins

Collins lives with her husband and two daughters on a 120 acre farm where they raise geese and ducks, as well as keep cats, dogs, hogs and 10 quarter horses. She has sewn since she was a little girl, making dolls and quilts. Nine or 10 years ago she began creating hand appliqued pictures after reading an article in *Better Homes and Gardens* about making machine-stitched pictures. Collins told herself "I don't get along with a sewing machine... but I can do that by hand" and has made 64 since then.

"I can't tell someone how to do this. First it comes out of your head, then you've got to sew real good," says the artist. Her ideas come from her imagination, poems, or others' suggestions. She does not work from a picture but may do some research for details. If people do not like what she has done, her attitude is: send it back. They need to be happy and she needs to be happy. "I am doing what I like," she says, "things are not perfect on this ol' farm - I dream of places ... what I would like to do ... what would be fun for me." An outdoor person, Collins mostly sews when everyone is asleep. She concentrates on outdoor scenes, farms, and an occasional small town. She likes repeated elements, small patterns in her materials (though she is using more solid colors now), and finds some things, such as water, difficult to capture.

■ 9. *What God Hath Promised*, 1990
fabric
35 x 44
Lent by Dr. Marsha Howell,
Little Rock

10. *The Witching Hour*, 1991
fabric
33 3/4 x 43 1/2
Lent by Dr. & Mrs. Ed Barron,
Little Rock

James Cottey

A native Arkansan, Cottey, has had a restless spirit. In college he studied engineering, sociology, and industrial arts. He recieved a masters degree in Education from the University of Arkansas, did some teaching, worked for his father's frozen food business and the University of Arkansas for Medical Sciences. He eventually taught drafting and crafts in Helena for five years.

"I was overwhelmed in 1970 when The Arkansas Arts Center brought in the Objects U.S.A. exhibition," says Cottey, "It inspired me to want to build in a contemporary direction." There he saw new possibilities in the work of Sam Maloof and Wendell Castle. Feeling his design skills were lacking, he enrolled in Virginia Commonwealth University where he studied with Alphonse Mattia, and was influenced by the 19th century furniture maker Thonet and the Art Nouveau style. Upon returning to Arkansas in 1975, Cottey and his wife purchased land near Shirley. They built their own home nestled in the side of a hill and converted a barn into a studio. His first works were extremely sculptural, but he soon found that was time consuming and financially unrewarding. Everything he does is unique and original and he prefers to work for himself. He despises making multiple parts, such as the legs of a table, but he likes to enhance the grain of the wood and is known for the sinuous silhouette.

■ 11. *Music Stand*, 1990
padauk, macassar ebony
60 3/4 x 24 1/4 x 33 - stand
25 x 25 1/4 x 17 - bench

12. *Sawhorses*, 1989
cherry, bubinga
28 x 47 1/4 x 20 1/2 each
The Arkansas Arts Center Foundation Collection

David & Becki Dahlstedt

The Mountain View Pottery (formerly American Beauty Pottery) and the Dahlstedts are one. David came to Arkansas with his parents at the age of three. His first introduction to clay was at Henderson State University with Joe Coulter, but it was not until he traveled and saw potteries in California that he realized he could make a living from the medium. After a short stint at the Dryden Pottery in Hot Springs, David took a position at the Ozark Folk Art Center in Mountain View and has been there since 1978. He has made one of a kind pieces for a long time, but found it was time consuming and unrewarding and has turned more and more to traditional pottery over the years.

Becki joined him eight years ago. She organizes, does the bookkeeping and monitors inventory; he orders supplies and fixes equipment. Both throw, decorate, sign their own pots and fire the kilns. His works are larger and the proportions are more generous; hers are smaller and lighter. Since 1992 they have impressed their work with "Made in Arkansas". Their production pottery is uniformly white with floral brush work in dashes of blue, green and red. David began producing his one of a kind leaning pitchers four or five years ago. They are a study in thrown and extruded construction and balance. The couple does 30 to 40 firings a year with 200 to 300 pieces per firing.

David Dahlstedt

■ 13. *Untitled*, 1993
   clay, glaze
   24 1/2 x 24 1/2 x 4 3/4

14. *Teapot*, 1993
   clay, slip, glaze
   7 3/4 x 10 x 6 1/4 all over

15. *Covered Baking Dish*, 1993
   clay, slip, glaze
   5 3/4 x 13 1/2 diameter

Becki Dahlstedt

16. *Fluted Bowl*, 1993
   clay, slip, glaze
   6 1/2 x 13 1/4 diameter

■ 17. *Soup Bowl with Saucer*, 1993
   clay, slip, glaze
   5 7/8 diameter - bowl
   7 diameter - saucer

Stephen Driver

"My life is drifting into things backward," says Driver. He attended Florida State University on an athletic scholarship to study psychology and became a potter. A kiln building workshop at the University of California, Davis set him in his current direction. There he could identify himself with the energy of a California potter who had formerly been a football player. Through family he was able to work at the Mark of the Potter production studio in Clarksville, Georgia. Then he worked in England under Michael Leach. After three months, with the help of friends, he was able to apprentice with traditional wood-firing English potters, Peter and Jill Dick. He returned to the United States in 1976 and with his brothers bought property near Oark as part of a back to the land adventure. Living in a tent, he and his wife, Louise Halsey, a weaver, started from scratch.

He returned to the University of Georgia for his M.F.A. degree and determined he was not production minded. He feels vessels, especially teapots, are architectural forms and that the spiral is a natural outcome of working on the potter's wheel. Working within the limitations of function is, for him, seductive. Driver avoids surface decoration and likes to push forms that are experimental and yet retain a strong connection with his materials and wood firing process.

- **18.** *Teapot*, 1993
   stoneware, wood-fired
   14 1/2 x 10 1/4 x 8

19. *Bowl*, 1993
   stoneware, wood-fired
   6 x 15 diameter

20. *Vase*, 1993
   stoneware, wood-fired
   6 1/2 x 8 1/2 x 3 3/8

Michael Haley & Susy Siegele

Haley and Siegele met in 1974 in Denton, Texas. He had studied business at the University of Texas and transferred to North Texas State University to work in clay and welded steel. She attended Texas Woman's University to study ceramics. While attending school they were selling pottery. That experience taught them resourcefulness and survival skills. While Haley held a job with the Dallas County Historical Society he came up with the idea of making blocks of colored clay. Weighing up to 200 pounds, these blocks are sliced cross-wise into slabs used to build functional forms.

They were introduced to Arkansas when a friend loaned them his hunting cabin in the Ozarks. They loved the mountains and the fog and were very much under the influence of oriental art at the time. The couple moved into their house/studio in 1983 and at the same time moved from a retail to a wholesale market. Today the Buzzard Mountain Pottery has five employees including Haley and Siegele and they are not looking for more accounts. Their work employs geometric patterns, faces and animals and Native American imagery. Their best markets are in Santa Fe, New Mexico; Washington, D.C.; Winston-Salem, North Carolina; and Yosemite, California. "We like a blend of styles, and a consistency of forms," says Haley, "the problem is that in standardizing your work it is difficult to introduce change."

21. *Two Lizards*, 1993
    colored porcelain
    1 x 13 1/4 x 13 1/4

22. *Yellow Striper*, 1993
    colored porcelain
    2 1/4 x 6 1/2 x 6 3/4

23. *Lizards on Stone*, 1993
    colored porcelain
    3 1/4 x 4 x 2 3/4

24. *Bowl*, 1993
    colored porcelain
    3 1/4 x 11 3/4 x 10 3/8

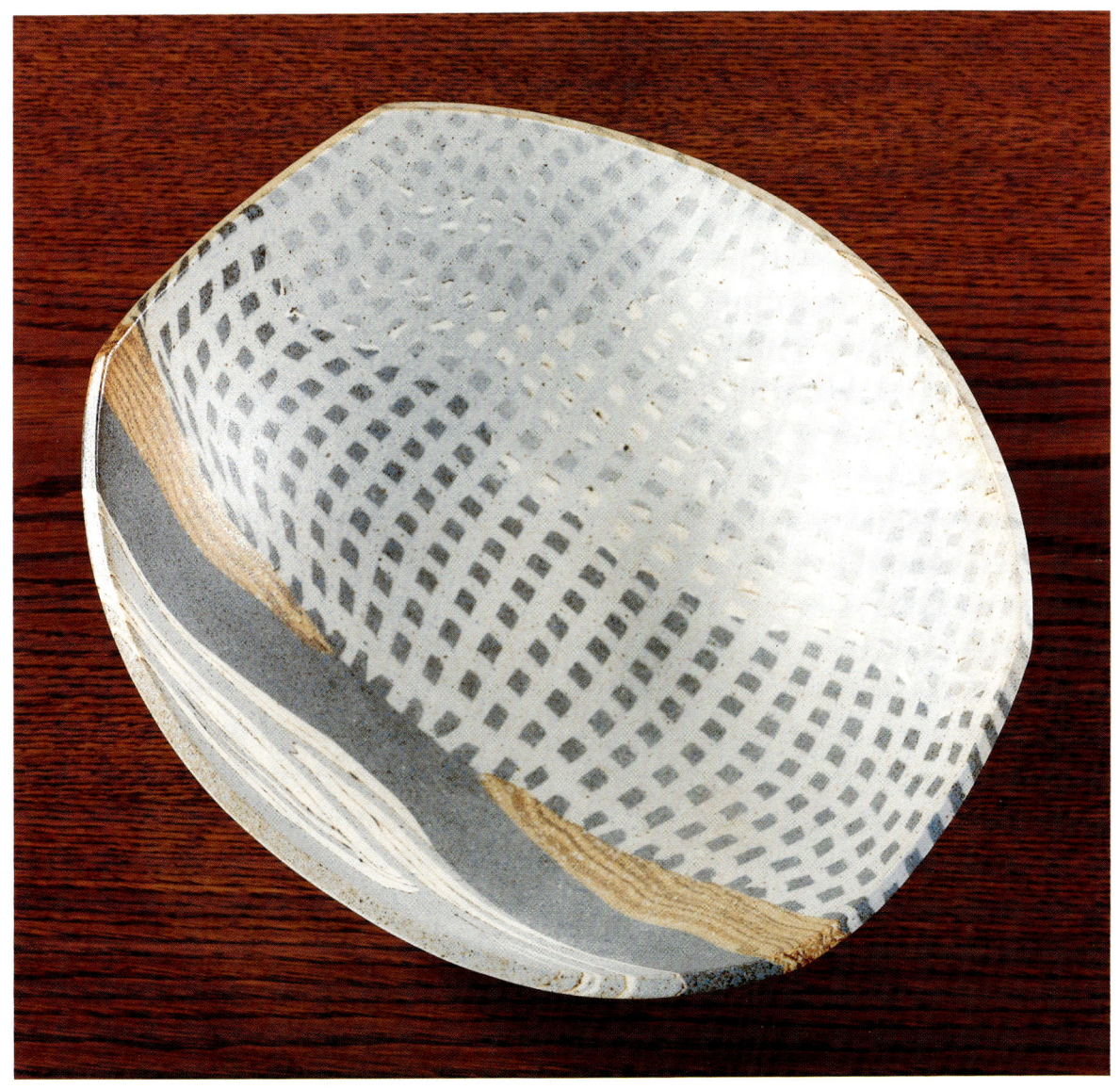

Thom Hall

A native Arkansan, Hall was especially influenced by his mother's ability to deal with everything in a creative way. If his parents gave him one lesson it was to do the things he wanted to do and to explore anything that interested him. At the University of Arkansas, Hall studied literature, speech and drama and the fine arts. "Fayetteville was a heavy hippie stronghold and involved an incredible mixture of people," recalls Hall, "in the late '60s and early '70s all of the barriers were down, people my age were rebellious and many who moved to Arkansas wanted to do something with their hands."

His first introduction to enameling was in Fayetteville, but the real impetus after college was at the Arts Center. In 1975 the enamelist William Harper gave a cloisonne workshop. The brilliant color, working on a flat surface and the instant feedback enticed him. Hall realized he could explore his interest in figurative images. Hall's work is autobiographical and mixes literary themes, fantasy, humor and the association to people in his family. He takes risks with his medium and is currently working to burn out the cloisonnes and is also using foil on copper to enhance color. To him color and light are the most important elements. Hall works to keep the color loose through fluid overlays and is looking for motion and a softer interpretation.

25. *Gloria - M.S. Jimmie Sue Bo Bo*, 1988
    cloisonne enamel on fine silver
    4 x 5
    Lent by Phyllis and Edward M. Kaplan, Memphis, Tennessee

■ 26. *Julie's Biscayne Boys*, 1989
    cloisonne enamel on fine silver
    4 x 5
    Lent by Andre Simon, Little Rock

27. *Beach Boy Water Play*, 1992
    cloisonne enamel on fine silver
    5 x 5

28. *Beach Shower: One Canary Speedo*, 1993
    cloisonne enamel on copper with silver foil, multiple high fire burn-out
    5 3/4 x 4 7/8

Irma Gail Hatcher

Hatcher grew up in Texas where, it seemed, if you could not draw a horse you could not be an artist. She chose sewing and cooking in school instead. In her 10th year she resolved to win a college scholarship through her sewing - vowing she would do anything to win. She won and attention to detail has been her hallmark ever since. Ten years ago she made her first quilts. The main reason was to decorate - antique quilts were too expensive. The Ohio Star was her first pattern but after seeing the works of Mary Jo Dalrymple and Mary Morgan she realized it was possible to design her own quilt.

In the past 10 years Hatcher has completed as many quilts, mostly for family. None have been for sale. She continues to use traditional patterns, but will analyze and manipulate them to her satisfaction. For her, structure comes first, color second. She prefers printed fabric rather than solids and she confesses that sometimes through the middle of a project she wonders what she has gotten into. Quilt making provides no immediate gratification. It is a matter of perseverance. Hatcher is thinking of making smaller works that are less time intensive so she can explore more ideas. Her biggest thrill is to enter a work in a competiton and to see it hanging. Hatcher now conducts workshops and lectures on quilting.

■ **29.** *Conway Album (I'm Not From Baltimore)*, 1992
cotton
90 x 90

Sharon Heidingsfelder

Heidingsfelder got her determination and grit from her mother and her construction ability from her father. In college she took home economics and interior design - she wanted to be the best interior designer in the world. Out of school, she quickly abandoned her major; she enrolled in the University of Tennessee and there was no question that it was crafts she wanted to study. It was Marian Heard, her teacher and the founder of Arrowmont School of Arts and Crafts in Gatlinburg, Tennessee, who sent her to Arkansas to work as a craft specialist for the state Cooperative Extension Service.

Heidingsfelder got into quilting because "I am cheap" she says, "Germans are frugal," and she wanted to decorate her house. She took a course with Nancy Crow at Arrowmont and was delighted to discover that she could design a quilt without having to do the actual quilting. Getting into the Quilt National with her first quilt was all the encouragement she needed. She has made 11 quilts in eight years. One of her challenges is to construct a quilt out of blocks that cannot be perceived as blocks. Every quilt has black and white stripes, which Heidingsfelder believes makes the other colors more vibrant. She enjoys geometric designs, but is beginning to work with curves. "Making a quilt is not the pleasant aspect," she says, "I love the result."

■ **30.** *Moongem of Paradise*, 1993
fabric, hand dyed
80 x 80 1/2

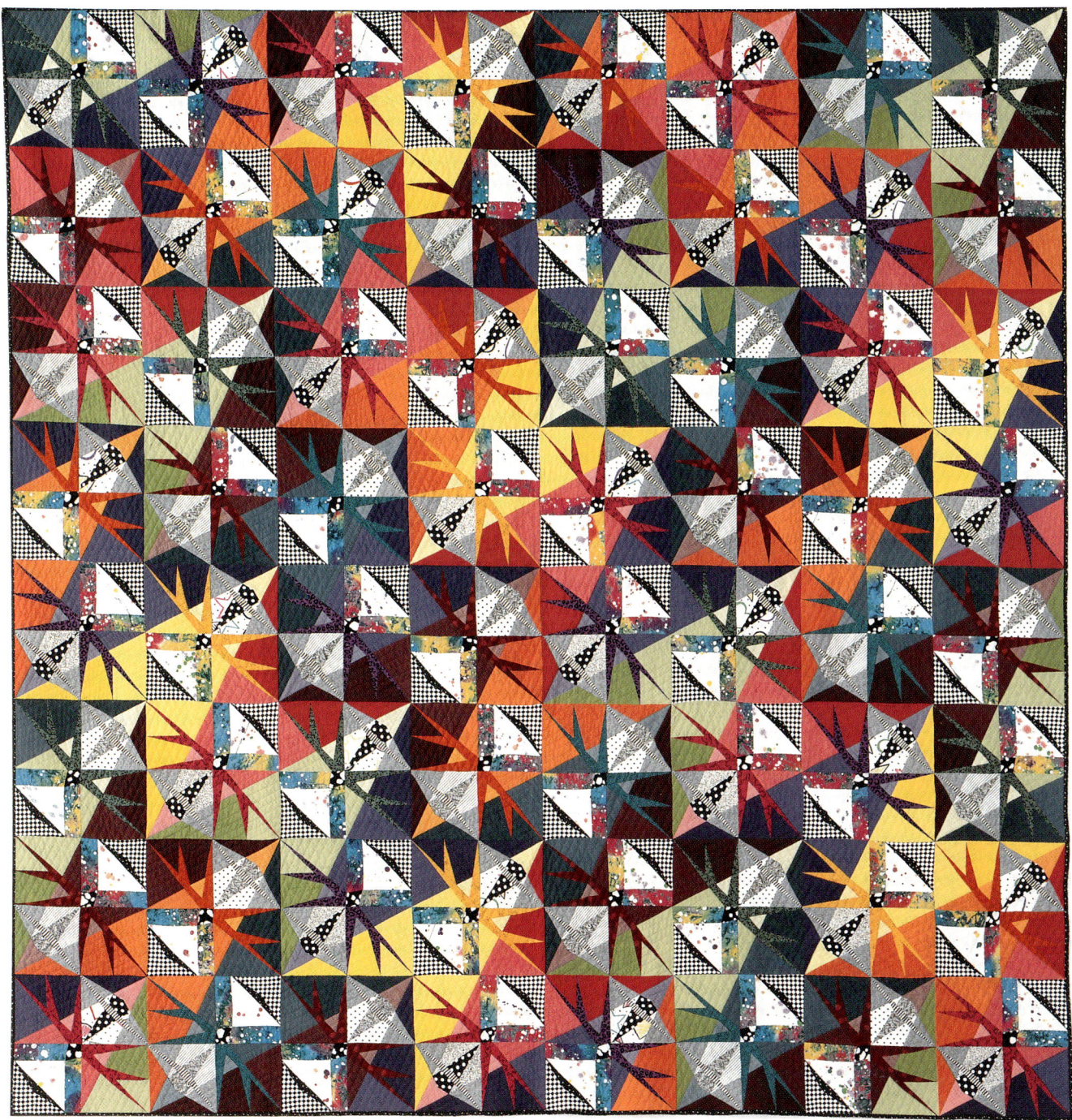

Robyn Horn

Horn was brought up in an art atmosphere and was an art major in college. She did photography for the state but soon felt that was rather mundane. In 1981 her brother-in-law, Sam Horn, took a wood-turning workshop with David Ellsworth at Arrowmont School of Arts and Crafts in Gatlinburg, Tennessee. When he returned "Sam had the tools - we had the shop," says Robyn, "Man that looked like fun - I fell into it - it felt right and was something to sink your teeth into."

After turning progessively more difficult forms, Horn began to look for something different and with her own stamp. She admired sculptor Isamu Noguchi and ceramist Graham Marks and the geode form. The form lends itself to variations in texture and contrast between smooth, rough, curved and angular areas. She introduced sliding dovetails in 1989 and is now considering faceting the surface more. She may incorporate rocks for bases and may even get invloved with large sandstone sculptures in the future. The figuration of wood is important. "I love pretty burl," she says, "and combining color is important to me." For her the process is important; she enjoys designing, but uses turning as a means to get to the finished piece, to which she responds in a visceral way. "The feeling you get when you look at a finished work and you know it's a good one is what I go for," says Horn, "It is what keeps you working."

31. ***Natural Bridge***, 1989
    redwood lace burl, lathe-turned, carved
    14 x 37

■ 32. ***On Ten Inch Centers***, 1991
    box elder burl, cocobolo, lathe-turned, routed
    13 x 19

Kaye Martinez

Born and educated in California, Martinez married and moved to Oregon where she was introduced to weaving on a 16th century back strap Inca loom at the university. She had long done needlepoint and learned batik during a year in Iran so upon returning to California she took a weaving course at San Jose State University. There she got hooked. She was ready to go into a graduate program when her husband's job brought the family to Arkansas in 1976. She was devasted to learn that no university offered courses in fiber. It took over a year for her to identify others working in the field. "Weaving is a solitary art form" says Martinez, "many times you feel you are the only person working in this medium." She also says it is only the strong who survive, "those with staying power; those [weaving] on the sidelines have dropped out."

Martinez works with on and off-loom techniques, making rugs, shawls and wall pieces. Color is important to her, but the design and technical pre-planning are the most enjoyable part. The thrill is in seeing the design slowly building on itself - emerging from nothing. She prefers natural fiber that is soft, tactile and rich in color. She has an 8-harness and a 16-harness loom with a manual dobby mechanism. She hopes one day to add a computer.

33. *Three Up*, 1993
knotless netting, wool
1 1/2 x 14 1/4 x 12 1/2

34. *Crossways*, 1993
wool, silk, hand-dyed
69 3/4 x 37 1/2

■ **35.** *Shawl #107*, 1992
silk, hand-dyed
95 x 22 3/4

Shep Miers

When Miers graduated with an M.F.A degree in sculpture, he found only four teaching jobs available in the country. So for five years he worked in student personnel and as assistant dean of students. Not satisfied being an administrator he thought there must be a way to use his training. He had enjoyed woodworking and began seeking out cabinet-making shops. Over a three and a half year period he apprenticed with two shops in Dallas - Manheim and Schieffer. Finally he said, "I bet I can do this."

He moved to Little Rock when his wife, Jane, took a residency at Children's Hospital in 1987. He made contact with interior designers and architects and has been making custom furniture ever since. He tries to balance this activity with his interest in elegant minimally curved sculpture. He tries to avoid trickery, admires Shaker furniture and feels what he does must have a lot of integrity. Miers' interests vary from Japanese packaging to architecture, from bicycle racing to sculling. He designed the cantilevered rocking chair in graduate school. In both furniture and sculpture he is concerned with minimal forms and balance, or implied balance, of color and mass. With furniture you "take the predetermined and use it to your advantage," he says.

36. *Variform*, 1986
  santos rosewood, birch
  98 x 10 5/8 x 3 3/4

■ **37.** *Rocker*, 1989
  walnut
  47 x 20 1/2 x 28
  Lent by Dan Hammitt, Dallas, Texas

Mary Morgan

Morgan grew up in the Ozarks, near Clinton. Art was not taught in the schools, so she took home economics and vividly recalls making her first dress out of printed feed sacks. She had two years of college before having to go to work. She has sewn since she was 10. She made clothes for herself and her daughter and always felt she had to change a pattern - had to do something different.

When blue jeans came into fashion, she had to find a creative outlet other than making clothes. Not knowing another soul who was quilting and finding only a few ideas in magazines, she forged ahead making her own quilts on a trial and error basis. She was eager to learn and actively sought kindred spirits which led to the founding of the Arkansas Quilters Guild in 1980. Shortly thereafter she was introduced to contemporary quilts with hand dyed fabrics. She got a chance to go to Arrowmont School of Arts and Crafts in Gatlinburg, Tennessee and study with Jan Meyer Newbury. It changed her life and opened up all sorts of possibilities. Morgan makes both traditional and contemporary quilts eight hours a day - often working on more than one at a time. Her designs incorporate one or two basic shapes repeated in sequence or in progression; the triangle is a popular element. For her the important thing is the process of making the quilt and to have fun manipulating brilliant, intense color.

■ **38.** *Pickety Stix-Red*, 1993
  fabric, hand-dyed
  41 x 46 7/8

John Mori

Mori has a background in small metal pieces, jewelry, ceramics, sculpture and bronze casting. Injuries to his hand and back and teaching at an institution without a foundry necessitated changing mediums. His approach to form is sculptural even though he feels his works lie between that of a potter and a furniture maker. Aside from doing site-specific pieces along the Arkansas River, his work over the past several years has been with a series of portals, gateways or passageways which he has been doing since he came to the state in 1986.

"The work I am doing now is probably more personal than anything I have ever done," says Mori. His Japanese-American background and growing up in New Mexico left him feeling isolated. The portal series relate to the internment his family faced during World War II, to his own identity and to decisions he has made. Temple gates are a direct influence but it is the choices in life and what governs those choices that he ponders, "choices that could have put you someplace very different." He has done more than two dozen portals and has lost count. He is sensitive to contrasting materials and colors and to scale. His works are poetic, quiet and reflective. "I don't know what makes my things relevant," said Mori, "the answers come from within you...the reasons are always changing."

■ **39. *Portal XXX*** , 1993
    clay, wood
    33 1/2 x 45 1/4 x 12 1/8

40. *Portal XXIV* , 1992
    paper, wood, thread
    19 7/8 x 59 1/4 x 23 3/4

Keith Newton

Newton's father owned a hardware store in Hampton, Arkansas and was the town's fix-it man so Keith had plenty of opportunity to work with tools and his dad was a good teacher. He studied business administration for 2 1/2 years before his money ran out and he started a leather shop selling hippie goods. That proved a dead end so he changed to carpentry and building houses. Gradually he acquired enough tools to set up a shop in Little Rock. In the late '70s he realized he had the ability to design - he could visualize the whole job. "I have good dreams," he said, "I make them come true with a certain amount of craftsmanship thrown in."

While Newton would like to work on speculation, he survives on custom work for individuals and corporations. The nature of his work is slow, requires up-front money for materials and any delay in a month's income could be disastrous. He hopes for clients who will give him free rein. He describes himself as a designer/craftsman and his work as contemporary with enough articulation of light and shade and detail to keep it interesting. Newton feels he is up against the client who must choose between his unique work that will take time to create or a manufactured product that costs less and is immediately available. He feels his back is always to the wall.

■ 41. *Side Table*, 1992
bubinga, wenge
30 x 70 x 20
Lent by Chris & Dana Durney,
Little Rock

42. *Vessel*, 1992
black gum (tupelo)
10 x 12 diameter
Dr. and Mrs. Rennie Bressinck,
Little Rock

Leon & Sharon Niehues

Leon and Sharon come from Midwestern backgrounds: his was a farming family of six boys in Kansas, hers was an Illinois banking family who lived east of St. Louis. Leon had dropped out of college and met Sharon in Topeka, Kansas; they had their honeymoon in Arkansas. Moving to this state was part of the back to the land movement in the middle '70s. Land was cheap and they reasoned that if they could work together with their hands and do exceptional work, their efforts would be rewarded. The incentive for making baskets was to earn an income. The first years were difficult.

They began with the aim of improving on traditional forms. In 1987 they branched out with more elaborate handles and patterns, which, in turn, led to their signature overlay technique. "We consider this work traditional," says Leon. Their works are simple, clean, strong, visually inviting and tactile. No one has to be educated to their vessels, they say, their language is universal. Basket making embodies the tension of their two personalities coming together. This tension is balanced in their baskets. The uprights are strong and masculine - Leon's preference. The weavers are small and feminine to accommodate small hands and provide smooth curves - Sharon's preference. "We have had to learn to work together," says Sharon.

■ **43.** *Peake*, 1991
   white oak, coralberry, waxed linen thread
   13 x 15 diameter

44. *Ring-handled Pot*, 1992
   white oak, waxed linen thread
   9 x 11 diameter

45. *Vireo*, 1993
   white oak, coralberry, waxed linen thread
   11 x 11 diameter

Ed & Amy Pennebaker

The Pennebakers met at the Hale Farm and Village in Bath, Ohio; he was in the glass blowing shop, she was in the pottery shop. Both majored in art in college. A high school teacher in Liberal, Kansas had taught Ed to blow glass. Amy majored in enameling. When they realized their employer was selling their glass to the Smithsonian Institution they decided they could make it own their own. They moved to Salem, Arkansas in 1985 and set up shop along Highway 62 with the intention to build a wholesale business and also retail to tourists. The tourists, however, did not stop so in 1991 they purchased a modern studio with access to a gas line and turned completely to wholesale.

As a production glass house they make 8,000 to 10,000 hand blown pieces a year. They specialize in Early American glass: tableware, drinking vessels, perfume bottles and ornaments, which market well on the East Coast. The bodies of the pieces are thinner than authentic Early American glass and are signed with an "E" and an "A" for Early American or for Ed and Amy. Their colors are: cobalt, teal green, aquamarine and amethyst, though other colors have been used in the past. Four years ago they incorporated as Red Fern Glass after the book *Where the Red Fern Grows*, by Wilson Rawls, a story about two dogs who need each other to work effectively. This summarizes their philosophy.

46. *Vase*, 1993
blown glass
6 3/4 x 3 1/2 diameter

47. *Swirled Bottle*, 1993
blown glass
5 3/4 x 2 3/4 diameter

48. *Chestnut Bottle*, 1993
blown glass
8 x 5 1/2 x 3 1/8

■ **49.** *Covered Sugar*, 1993
blown glass
8 3/4 x 4 diameter all over

Helen Phillips

One of Phillips' favorite places to play as a child was a burial ground, which probably relates to her current interest in sacred places. She took to drawing naturally and wanted to be an art teacher. She actually began teaching before graduating in 1961. Four years later she traveled with her husband to Okinawa and studied with a potter who had a working relationship with Hamada. Other travels followed: Germany, Hawaii, Santa Barbara, California and Birmingham, Alabama. In 1974 she received a teaching assistantship at the University of Florida. She has been teaching at the University of Central Arkansas since 1976.

Six years ago a mid-life crisis led Phillips to therapy, Jungian psychology, work with her dreams and the study of African art. Since then her art has become personal and, she reasons, if it can be therapeutic for her, then it can be for viewers as well. She has had the opportunity to study megaliths in Ireland and received a travel grant to the Ivory Coast, where she "found a living connection to the very primitive source of art as a transforming magical activity both for the artist and the viewer." Her motifs include the house, platforms, fish and crucibles. "They represent my life," she says. They are sacred and mysterious places that relate to her many inner selves.

50. ***It seemed that they were watching***, 1993
    clay, silver leaf, raku-fired
    Left: 19 1/2 x 12 3/4 x 3 3/4
    Right: 19 x 12 3/4 x 3 1/2

51. ***...and they flew straight up***, 1993
    clay, silver leaf, raku-fired
    58 x 11 x 13

Laura Phillips

She is Helen Phillips' daughter and was exposed to art everywhere her parents traveled, but was bored by the whole scene. When she went to college she had no intention of following art, but a year in Japan studying the language, tea ceremony, calligraphy and pottery changed her mind. She completed her undergraduate studies in art and Asian studies. After a summer clay program at Alfred University in New York and a workshop with Jun Kaneko, she applied and was accepted for graduate studies at Cranbrook Academy in Michigan. Her biggest lesson there, she says, was learning to go into the studio and work 70 hours a week. Since graduation she has taught at two universities and now teaches independently.

Phillips talks of having to work through problems. She expresses an interest in hand-building techniques, impressionistic surface manipulation and particularly enjoys the matte colors of low fire glazes. In her work she depicts animals and people with a child-like innocence and spontaneity. "That child is still operating," she says, but the "child's energy is being channeled by an adult." She goes on to explain that for her there is always a struggle to have the material and the idea meet on equal footing so neither is overwhelmed by or inadequate to the other. She tends to work in series and the most recent work is beginning to incorporate written messages.

■ **52.** *We Need an Operation*, 1992
    ceramic, salt-glazed
    16 x 10 1/2 x 11

53. *Little Girl*, 1993
    ceramic, raku-fired
    15 x 13 x 2

Liz Powers

In college, Powers majored in commercial art and minored in French. She married immediately after graduation. Inspired by her father, a Little Rock surgeon who took up painting at age 52, she worked at home, raising her family, and kept up her interest in art by doing commissions in oil from time to time. The family moved to Benton in 1967 and stayed there for 15 years. She began to tire of doing commissions and joined a friend in taking an enameling course at The Arkansas Arts Center and fell in love with the process.

Today, Powers is equally versatile in drawing, painting and enameling and is reluctant to put all of her energies into one medium, believing that events have a way of steering one's life. She does not accept enameling commissions so her work here is a little more independent of outside limitations. She is attracted to color, loves fantasy and old religious works, likes things in balance and avoids any feeling of discord. "I am a mother and mediator," she explains. A characteristic of enameling she likes is cutting the metal and giving it form that cannot be given to painting. "I want to do something and have people say 'How did she do that,'" she says, "I want to teach people that this is a neat, neat medium." "I want to keep growing - we all do."

54. *Celestial and Charge*, 1993
    cloisonne enamel on fine silver,
    gold & silver foil
    6 x 7

55. *John in the Dining Room*, 1993
    cloisonne enamel on fine silver,
    gold & silver foil
    6 1/4 x 6 3/4

■ 56. *Guardian with Yellow Wings*, 1993
    cloisonne enamel on fine silver,
    gold & silver foil
    5 diameter

Owen Rein

Rein moved to Arkansas for specific reasons: the oaks and hickories that grow here and being able to live without much money or too many rules and restrictions. Back East he had a struggle getting started. To economize, he and his wife lived in a tent while building their first 7-by-14-foot cabin for under $600. They were squatters. Their second cabin was bigger and they realized that the earlier experience not only had eliminated their bills, but with jobs enabled them to save $25,000 over a three-year-period.

During that time Rein was already making furniture. What he made was expensive to produce, requiring power tools, materials, a big shop, overhead and capital. The "Fox Fire" books of the '70s showing the type of work people did in backwoods areas gave him the idea that he could make a chair with hand tools and with minimum overhead as long as he had direct access to materials. He picked chairs because, like tires, everybody needs them. His original plan was simple, make and sell one chair a week for $75 and there would be enough to live on. He also felt that within these limitations he could do superior work. "I don't go for rustic at all," he said. "First and foremost I am trying to make a good chair. I think of my chairs as being sophisticated."

■ **57.** ***Rocking Chair***, 1993
 oak, hickory
 47 1/4 x 24 x 34 1/2

58. ***Dining Chair***, 1993
 oak, hickory
 45 x 19 x 16 1/2

Douglas Stowe

Stowe studied political science at a Presbyterian college in Nebraska and came out a conscientious objector. He was a member of the counter culture movement and says he still has leanings in that direction. He moved to Eureka Springs from Memphis in 1975 and joined a pottery cooperative. When he found he was the only one paying the bills, he moved to making furniture out of barn wood. That enterprise went bankrupt and by taking commissions from his friends, who he said went out on a limb for his sake, he was able to continue in woodworking. "I gave them the very best," he said, "more than they expected." Today most of his customers can be traced to those central few.

Stowe is noted for his custom made chest-of-drawers which he designs with suggestions from his clients and proportions intuitively. He also has a production line of small boxes that are pieced and glued with a variety of woods - all are found within 50 miles of his shop. An environmentalist, he is opposed to the rampant depletion of exotic woods from Third World countries. In the future he would like to help people in other countries learn to work their wood using American technology and thus reverse their countries' outflow of raw materials.

■ **59.** ***Jewelry Box***, 1993
curly maple
12 3/4 x 10 1/4 x 7 1/4

60. ***Writing Desk in Tribal Theme***,
1993
ebonized cherry, bird's-eye maple
36 x 38 x 24

Mark Werner

The landscape may have something to do with Werner's leaning toward sculpture since moving to Arkansas in 1977. He finds that the woods are so lush and plentiful that he is excited about going out and directly gathering the materials he uses. Knowing he didn't want to teach after graduating from art school, Werner's father offered his son the opportunity to live at his vacation home, essentially to keep it from being burglarized. Later, he and his wife built their own home on that land. He says isolation is not new to him, his parents often took vacations to remote places.

Werner does lattice-like wall constructions, paints and draws. His three-dimensional work involves a constant ordering and tension of materials as can be seen in the tight grids he weaves from freshly cut vines. "I try to keep function and idea separate," he says, "I don't want to say I am making something - a chair or a bowl." He feels his relationship to craft is akin to the process he uses, particularly going out and gathering his own natural materials. For him the work suggests ancient and primitive cultures. "I like to allude to things without loading up on them," he said.

■ **61.** *Darwin's Gate*, 1992
various woods
58 1/2 x 43 5/8 x 7 1/2

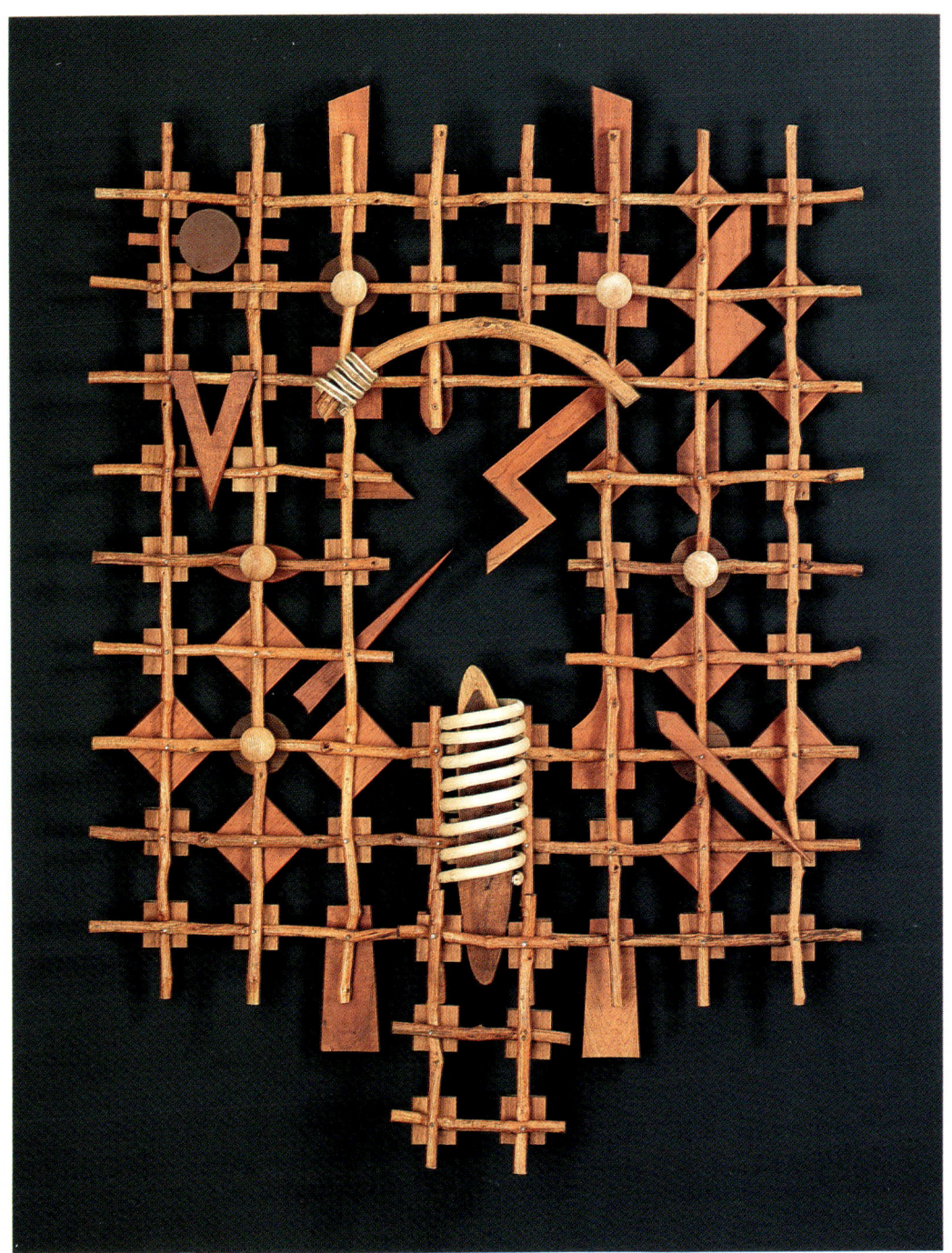

Biographies

Gayle Batson

801 N. Jackson Street
Little Rock, Arkansas 72205

Born: Fayetteville, Arkansas, 1951

Education: B.A. (art), University of Arkansas, Fayetteville; Philbrook Arts Center, Tulsa, Oklahoma; The Arkansas Arts Center Museum School, Little Rock; Graduate studies at Arrowmont School of Arts and Crafts, University of Tennessee, Gatlinburg; workshops with Catherine Heirsioux, Harvey Sadow, Toshiko Takaezu, Don Pilcher

Exhibitions: 1992 - "35th Annual Delta Exhibition," The Arkansas Arts Center, Little Rock; 1991 - "Rituals and Primitive Origins," Sarratt Gallery, Vanderbilt University, Nashville, Tennessee; 1990 - "Sculpture/Drawing Invitational Exhibition," Hendrix College, Conway, Arkansas; "18th Annual Toys Designed by Artists," The Arkansas Arts Center, Little Rock; 1985 - "18th Annual Prints, Drawings and Crafts Exhibition," The Arkansas Arts Center, Little Rock

Collections: Sanford M. and Diane Besser Collection, Little Rock; Hendrix College, Conway, AR; First Commercial Bank, Little Rock; Mitchell, Selig, Gates & Woodyard, Little Rock; University of Arkansas at Pine Bluff; Phyllis George Brown, Frankfort, KY; Dr. I. Dodd & Virginia Wilson, Little Rock; University of Arkansas for Medical Sciences, Little Rock; Elizabeth Willis-Sowards, Wichita, KS; The Arkansas Arts Center Foundation Collection, Little Rock

Related Professional Experience: Pottery instructor, The Arkansas Arts Center, 1979 - present; children's visual arts instructor, The Arkansas Arts Center, 1976-1988; art instructor, University of Arkansas at Little Rock, 1977-1978; workshops, 1974 - present

David Blaisus

(works with Jeanmarie Rain Mako)
Classic Oak Baskets
HCR 72 Box 67
Parthenon, Arkansas 72666

Born: Cloquet, Minnesota, 1959

Awards/Honors: Fellowship, Arkansas Arts Council, 1992

Education: University of Minnesota; workshop with Doug McDougal
    Self taught

Exhibitions: 1991 - "Basketry from all Directions," Arrowmont School of Arts and Craft, Gatlinburg, TN; 1990 - "Basketweave '90," Dairy Barn Arts Center, Athens, OH

Joe Bruhin

Fox Mountain Pottery
Route 64 West, Box 247-B
Fox, Arkansas 72051

Born: St. Louis, Missouri, 1953

Awards/Honors: Fellowship, Arkansas Arts Council, 1992

Education: Idaho State University, Pocatello; Maryville College, St. Louis, Missouri (studied with Jeri Au); Meremac Community College, Kirkwood, Missouri (studied with Bob Allen)

Exhibitions: 1992 - "Regional Craft Biennial," The Arkansas Arts Center, Little Rock; 1983 - "Vessel Aesthetics," Taft College Art Gallery, California

Collections: Private collections in Missouri, Tennessee and Arkansas

Nancy Jane Collins

800 Creek Road
Floral, Arkansas 72534

Born: Searcy, Arkansas, 1956

Education: McClellan High School, Little Rock
    Self taught

Exhibitions: 1990 - Solo exhibition, Arkansas Territorial Restoration, Little Rock; 1988 - Solo exhibition, Stevens Art Gallery, Harding University, Searcy, Arkansas

Collections: Dr. & Mrs. Edwin Barron, Little Rock; Dr. Marsha Howell, Little Rock; Little Rock Public Library; State of Arkansas

Publications: Pohl, Kathy, "Country Stitchin," *Country Woman*, Spring 1990; Eitel, Jean, "Farmscapes in Fabric," *Quilts*, Spring, 1988, p. 15

James Cottey

HC 63, Box 311
Clinton, Arkansas 72031

Born: Little Rock, Arkansas, 1939

Education: M.F.A., Virginia Commonwealth University, Richmond; M.Ed., University of Arkansas, Fayetteville; B.Ed., Arkansas A & M College, Monticello

Exhibitions: 1988 - "Regional Craft Biennial," The Arkansas Arts Center, Little Rock; "Clay and Wood: Helen Phillips & James Cottey," The Arkansas Arts Center, Little Rock; two person exhibition, Arkansas Territorial Restoration, Little Rock; 1985 - "18th Annual Prints, Drawings and Crafts Exhibition," The Arkansas Arts Center, Little Rock; "National Furniture Exhibition," Itawamba Junior College, Tupelo, Mississippi

Collections: Myra Beatty, Akron, OH; Herb Rule III, Little Rock; Dr. I. Dodd & Virginia Wilson, Little Rock; The Arkansas Arts Center Foundation Collection, Little Rock

Related Professional Experience: Workshop "Creativity in Art," Arkansas Tech University, Russellville, 1989

Publications: Fine Woodworking Design Book Two, (Taunton Press, Inc.: Newtown, CT) 1987; Handcrafted Shelves & Cabinets,(Rodale Press: New Jersey), 1984; "Now America Craft" Craft Horizons (American Craft Council, New York) 1974

Becky Dahlstedt

(works with David Dahlstedt)
HC 73 Box 8
Mountain View, Arkansas 72560

Born: Cape Girardeau, Missouri, 1945

Education: B.A. (art, English, French), Southeast Missouri State University

Exhibitions: 1989 - two person exhibition, Arkansas Territorial Restoration, Little Rock; 1987 - "Potters Platters," organized by Ozark Regional Craft Association, venues included Harding University, Searcy, AR; University of the Ozarks, Clarksville, AR; University Museum, University of Arkansas, Fayetteville; Arkansas Territorial Restoration, Little Rock

Related Professional Experience: Crafts interpreter, Ozark Folk Center, Mountain View, Arkansas, 1986 - present

Publications: Thompson, J.J., "Arkansas: Her Beauty and Character" (August House: Little Rock) 1989, pp. 79-80.

David Dahlstedt

(works with Becky Dahlstedt)
HC 73 Box 8
Mountain View, Arkansas 72560

Born: Lincoln, Nebraska, 1951

Awards/Honors: Fellowship, Arkansas Arts Council, 1989

Education: B.A. (art), Henderson State University, Arkadelphia, Arkansas

Exhibitions: 1990 - "Regional Craft Biennial," The Arkansas Arts Center, Little Rock; 1988 - "Regional Craft Biennial," The Arkansas Arts Center, Little Rock; 1987 - "Potters Platters," organized by Ozark Regional Craft Association, venues included Harding University, Searcy, AR; University of the Ozarks, Clarksville, AR; University Museum, University of Arkansas, Fayetteville; Arkansas Territorial Restoration, Little Rock

Collections: The Arkansas Arts Center Foundation Collection, Little Rock

Related Professional Experience: Crafts interpreter, Ozark Folk Center, Mountain View, Arkansas, 1978 - present; Workshop, The Arkansas Arts Center Museum School, Little Rock, 1992

Publications: See Becky Dahlstedt

Stephen Michael Driver

HCR 61, Box 139
Ozark, Arkansas 72949

Born: Seattle, Washington, 1951

Education: M.F.A. (ceramics), University of Georgia, Athens; B.A. (Psychology), Florida State Unversity, Tallahassee; Penland School of Crafts workshop - iron forging; Penland School of Crafts - studied with Terry Allen, Tom Suomolainen, Don Reitz; Grass Valley, California, workshops with Richard Hotchkiss, Rimas Visgirda, Joel Goodkind, Doug Tweed

Exhibitions: 1993 - "Ceramics Southeast," University of Georgia Fine Arts Gallery, Athens; "Clay and Fiber," Octagon Center for the Arts, Ames, IA; 1992 - "Regional Craft Biennial," The Arkansas Arts Center, Little Rock; "Feats of Clay V," Lincoln Arts Center, CA; 1991 - group exhibition, University of Central Arkansas, Conway; two person exhibition, University of the Ozarks, Clarksville, AR; 1990 - two person exhibition, University of Arkansas at Little Rock; "Fifth Annual Monarch Tile National Ceramic Competition," San Angelo Museum of Fine Arts, Texas; 1989 - "Craftsman's Guild of Mississippi Invitational," Mississippi Museum of Art, Jackson; "Fourth Annual Monarch Tile National Ceramic Competition," San Angelo Museum of Fine Arts, TX

Collections: Lamar Dodd Art Center, LaGrange, GA; Ed & June Freeman, Pine Bluff, AR; Maurice Sendak, Ridgefield, CT

Related Professional Experience: Artist in Residence, Southern Arkansas University, Magnolia, March - May, 1993; Artist in Residence, Pocahontas High School, AR, January through February, 1993; workshop at The Arkansas Arts Center Museum School, April, 1993

Galleries: The Farrell Collection, Washington, D.C.; A. Houberbocken, Inc., Milwaukee, WI

Michael Haley

(works with Susy Siegele)
Buzzard Mountain Studios
Route 5 Box 129-b
Huntsville, Arkansas 72740

Born: Pittsburg, Texas, 1947

Education: M.A., Texas Woman's University - Denton; B.S. (business), North Texas State University - Denton
   Self taught

Related Professional Experience: Workshops - "Colored Clays in Patterns," Dallas Craft Guild, TX; "Colored Clay," Osage Pottery, Berryville, AR; "Colored Porcelain at Tarrant County College," Fort Worth, TX; "Neriage Slab Construction," Cedar Valley College, Lancaster, TX

Galleries: Kent Galleries, Santa Fe, NM; Appalachian Spring, Washington, D.C.; Ansel Adams Gallery, Yosemite, CA

Thom Hall

1423 Center Street
Little Rock, Arkansas 72202

Born: Fayetteville, Arkansas, 1948

Education: University of Arkansas, Fayetteville; Workshops with William Harper, Cynthia Bringle, Patti Warashina, Robert Andrew Parker, Burton Callicott, Ted Faiers, Marcel Witkowski, Randall Timmons, Lowell Nesbitt

Exhibitions: 1991 - "21st Annual Prints, Drawings and Photographs Exhibition," The Arkansas Arts Center, Little Rock; 1989 - "Six Artists from Arkansas," Alice Bingham Gallery, Memphis, TN; "Two Decades of American Craft: From The Arkansas Arts Center Foundation Collection," Snow Fine Arts Center, University of Central Arkansas, Conway; 1988 - "31st Annual Delta Art Exhibition," The Arkansas Arts Center, Little Rock; "Regional Craft Biennial," The Arkansas Arts Center, Little Rock

Collections: David and Pam Banks, Fort Smith, AR; Sanford M. and Diane Besser Collection, Little Rock; Prudential Insurance, Bellaire, TX; Stephens, Inc., Little Rock; The Arkansas Arts Center Foundation Collection, Little Rock

Irma Gail Hatcher

916 Heather Circle
Conway, Arkansas 72032

Born: Fort Worth, Texas, 1938

Education: B.S. (elementary education), Baker University, Baldwin City, Kansas

Exhibitions: 1993 - "American Quilter's Society Show," Paducah, KY; 1992 - "American International Quilt Association Show," Houston, TX; "Regional Craft Biennial," The Arkansas Arts Center, Little Rock

Related Professional Experience: Workshops in Arkansas, Texas, New Mexico, Kansas, Missouri, Louisiana, Virginia, South Carolina and Oklahoma include: "Designing Your Own Quilts," "Quilting Techniques," "3-D Applique," "Color Workshop," "Raised Applique," "Boxed Roses"

Publications: Hatcher, Irma Gail, *Conway Album (I'm Not from Baltimore) Quilt: Patterns and Techniques for Prize-Winning Applique*, (American School of Needlework, Inc.: San Marcos, CA) 1992.

Sharon Heidingsfelder

8010 Dan Thomas Road
Little Rock, Arkansas 72206

Born: Johnstown, Pennsylvania, 1950

Education: M.S. (Crafts), University of Tennessee, Knoxville; B.S., The Pennsylvania State University, University Park; Arrowmont School of Arts and Crafts, Gatlinburg, Tennessee; University of Arkansas, Little Rock; University of Arizona, Tucson

Awards/Honors: Fellowship, Arkansas Arts Council, 1989

Exhibitions: 1993 - "Quilt National '93," Dairy Barn Art Center, Athens, OH; 1991 - "Contemporary Quilts USA," Boston University, MA, international tour; "Quilt National '91," The Dairy Barn Southeastern Ohio Cultural Arts Center, Athens; "Quilts as a New Art Form - A National Exhibition of 21 Contemporary Artists," Janis Wetsman 20th Century Decorative Art Gallery, Birmingham, MI; 1990 - "Southern Quilts: A New View," The Hunter Museum, Chattanooga, TN, national tour; "Long Island Quilter's Society 15th Annual Convention and Exhibit," Hofstra University, Hempstead, NY; "Regional Craft Biennial," The Arkansas Arts Center, Little Rock; "6th Annual American Quilter's Society Annual Show," Paducah, KY; 1989 - "Quilt National '89," The Dairy Barn Southeastern Ohio Cultural Arts Center, Athens

Collections: Lewis Kern, Sarasota, FL; The Arkansas Arts Center, Little Rock

Publications: Ramsey, B. and G.A. Trechsel. *Southern Quilts: A New View.* (EPM Publications: McLean, Virginia) 1991; *Award Winning Quilts & Their Makers, Vol. I: The Best of AQS Shows 1985-1987.* (Schroeder Publishing Co., Inc.: Paducah, Kentucky) 1991.; Klaric, A., Ed. *Contemporary Quilts USA*. Arts America, United States Information Agency and Boston University Art Gallery, 1990; Timby, D.B., Ed. *VISIONS, Quilts of a New Decade* (C&T Publishing: Lafayette, California) 1990.; Roe, N., ed. *NEW QUILTS: Interpretations and Innovations* (Schiffer Publishing Ltd: West Chester, Pennsylvania) 1989; Roe, N., ed., *Fiber Expressions, The Contemporary Quilt* (Schiffer Publishing Ltd: West Chester, Pennsylvania) 1987; Roe, N., and H. Panich, eds., *Quilts, The State of the Art* (Schiffer Publishing Ltd: West Chester, Pennsylvania)

Robyn Horn

7801 Westwood Avenue
Little Rock, Arkansas 72204

Born: Fort Smith, Arkansas, 1951

Education: B.A., Hendrix College, Conway, Arkansas

Exhibitions: 1993 - "Turned Wood," Hunter Museum, Chattanooga, TN; 1992 - "Out of the Woods: Turned Wood by American Craftsmen," Fine Arts Museum of the South, Mobile, AL; 1991 - "Challenge IV," Port of History Museum, Philadelphia, PA; 1990 - "Regional Craft Biennial," The Arkansas Arts Center, Little Rock; 1989 - "American Contemporary Works in Wood," The Dairy Barn, Athens, OH; 1988 - "International Turned Objects Show," Port of History Museum, Philadelphia, PA, national tour

Collections: Arrowmont School of Arts and Crafts, Gatlinburg, TN; Arkansas Psychology Associates, Little Rock; Beverly Enterprises, Pasadena, CA; Fine Arts Museum of the South, Mobile, AL; Halstead Industries, Inc., Greensboro, NC; Mason Collection, Washington, D.C.; Munro Industries, Hot Springs, AR; Rose Law Firm, Little Rock; Sutherland, Asbill and Brenner, Atlanta, GA; Wood Turning Center, Philadelphia, PA; Wornick Collection, Hillsborough, CA; The Arkansas Arts Center Foundation Collection, Little Rock

Publications: *Fine Woodworking Design Book Six* (Taunton Press: Newtown, Connecticut), 1992; *Out of the Woods: Turned Wood by American Craftsmen*, 1992; *Fine Woodworking Design Book Five* (Taunton Press: Newtown, Connecticut), 1990; International Turned Objects Show Catalog, pp. 44-45, 1988

Jeanmarie Rain Mako

(works with David Blaisus)
Classic Oak Baskets
HCR 72, Box 67
Parthenon, Arkansas 72666

Born: Lakeville, Minnesota, 1959

Education: University of Minnesota; St. Cloud University London program

Exhibitions: See David Blaisus

Kaye Martinez

1502 Quail Creek Drive
Conway, Arkansas 72032

Born: Grass Valley, California, 1946

Education: B.S. (business administration), California State, Fresno; Fiber studies with Michelle Wipplinger, Linda Knutsen, Karen Selk, Sharon Alderman, Else Regenskena, Anne Brooks, Junko Sato Pollack, Anita Mayer

Exhibitions: 1990-"Path of the Weaver," Memphis College of Art, Tennessee; 1984-"Fiber National '84," Adams Memorial Gallery, Dunkirk, NY

Collections: Bank of Cabot, AR; Mr. & Mrs. James Faulkner, Little Rock; Mr. & Mrs. Flavio Gerbolini, Lima, Peru; Mr. & Mrs. Paul Hammond, Sonora, CA; Mr. & Mrs. David Lea, Brevard, NC; Dr. & Mrs. Clarence Mannasmith, Morrilton, AR; Dr. & Mrs. Ned Raun, Falls Church, VA

Related Professional Experience: Workshops for Central Arkansas Weavers Guild, Little Rock

Shep Miers

CSM Design, Inc.
3016 S. Lewis Street
Little Rock, Arkansas 72204

Born: Magnolia, Arkansas, 1953

Education: M.F.A. (sculpture), University of Dallas, Texas; M.A. (sculpture), University of Dallas, Texas; B.A. (art), Southern Arkansas University, Magnolia

Awards/Honors: Fellowship, Arkansas Arts Council, 1992

Exhibitions: 1992 - solo exhibition, Conduit Gallery, Dallas, TX; 1989 - solo exhibition, Conduit Gallery, Dallas, TX; 1988 - solo exhibition, Arkansas Territorial Restoration, Little Rock; 1983 - solo exhibition, Midwestern State University, Wichita Falls, TX

Collections: Mr. Jon D. Forsyth, Jr., Midland, TX; Mr. Richard Gorienko, Calgary, Alberta, Canada; Mr. & Mrs. Scott Markham, Conway, AR; Mountain Valley Water, Hot Springs, AR; Southern Arkansas University, Magnolia; Southland Corporation, Dallas, TX; Mr. & Mrs. Richard Stevens, Little Rock; Mr. & Mrs. Juergen Strunck, Southlake, TX; Mr. & Mrs. Jeffry Vaughn, St. Louis, MO

Related Professional Experience: Woodworking instructor, The Arkansas Arts Center Museum School, Summer 1991

Gallery: Conduit Gallery, Dallas, TX

Mary Morgan

10203 Milkyway Drive
Little Rock, Arkansas 72209

Born: Jackson, Wyoming, 1935

Education: Arkansas State Teacher's College, Jonesboro
  Self taught

Awards/Honors: Fellowship, Arkansas Arts Council, 1992

Exhibitions: 1992-"Regional Craft Biennial," The Arkansas Arts Center; 1991-"Contemporary Quilts: Spirit of the '90s," Kalamazoo Institute of Arts, Michigan; "American Quilters Society Show," Paducah, KY; 1990 - "Regional Craft Biennial," The Arkansas Arts Center, Little Rock

Collections: Arkansas Rehabilitation Institute, Little Rock; Sanford M. and Diane Besser Collection, Little Rock; Dean Witter, Little Rock; First Commercial Bank, Little Rock; Barbara Graves Intimate Fashions, Little Rock; Philip Lyon Law Firm, Little Rock; Museum of the American Quilters Society, Paducah, KY; Senator & Mrs. David Pryor, Washington, D.C.

Publications: Hillary Fletcher, Ed. *The New Quilt I* (Taunton Press: Newtown, Connecticut) 1991

John Mori

Art Department
Arkansas Tech University
Russellville, Arkansas 72801

Born: Albuquerque, New Mexico, 1951

Education: M.F.A. (sculpture), Southern Illinois University at Carbondale; B.F.A. (ceramics and metalworking), University of New Mexico; apprenticed with Paul Sutzman, Albuquerque, New Mexico.

Awards/Honors: Research grant, Arkansas Tech University, 1989; fellowship, Arkansas Arts Council, 1992

Exhibitions: 1993 - "Twenty-Second Prints Drawings and Photographs Exhibition," The Arkansas Arts Center, Little Rock; "Scinthya Edwards/John Mori," University of Arkansas at Little Rock; 1992 - "Regional Craft Biennial," The Arkansas Arts Center, Little Rock; 1991 - "The Arkansas Collection: An Invitation," University of Arkansas at Little Rock; 1986 - "Cast in Carbondale IV," Memphis College of Art, TN, traveling show

Collections: Dr. Louise Blackwell, Memphis, TN; Roberto Bertoia, Ithaca, NY; Dr. Linda Bell, Russellville, AR; Judy and David Coomber, Memphis, TN; Fort Smith Art Center, AR; Patti Lechman, Memphis, TN; Ralph and Pam Moss, Memphis, TN; John Richardson, Carbondale, IL; Ester Siderman, Chicago, IL; University of Arkansas at Little Rock Law School; Wanda Gurley Wilson, Memphis, TN; Dr. Helen Walker, Memphis, TN; Susan Walker, Pensacola, FL; The Arkansas Arts Center, Little Rock.

Related Professional Experience: Assistant professor of art, Arkansas Tech University, Russellville, 1987 - present; Visiting instructor, Memphis College of Art, TN, 1985-1986; Artist in Residence, Shelby State Community College, Memphis, TN, 1983-1984; exhibitions designer, preparator, technician, National Ornamental Metal Museum, Memphis, TN, 1982-1984

Keith Newton

2307 Arch Street
Little Rock, Arkansas 72206

Born: Hampton, Arkansas, 1948

Awards/Honors: Fellowship, Arkansas Arts Council, 1992

Education: University of Arkansas, Fayetteville
  Self taught

Exhibitions: 1990 - "Regional Craft Biennial," The Arkansas Arts Center, Little Rock; 1982 - solo exhibition, Arkansas Territorial Restoration; 1981 - "Prints, Drawings and Crafts," The Arkansas Arts Center, Little Rock

Collections: Dr. & Mrs. Rennie Bressinck, Little Rock; Hillary Rodham Clinton, Washington, D.C.; Jane Dickey, Little Rock; Charles Hicks, Little Rock; Gary P. & Rosemarie Nunn, Little Rock; Tad Phillips, Little Rock; Herb Rule III, Little Rock

Leon Niehues

(works with Sharon Niehues)
Niehues Baskets
HCR 64, Box 50
Pettigrew, Arkansas 72752

Born: Seneca, Kansas, 1951

Awards/Honors: Fellowship, Arkansas Arts Council, 1992

Education: University of Kansas, Lawrence
  Self taught

Exhibitions: 1993 - "Summer Basketry Exhibition," Nancy Margolis Gallery, Portland, ME; Two-person exhibition, Brown/Grotta Gallery, Wilton, CT

Collections: Sanford M. and Diane Besser Collection, Little Rock; Hans & Margreth Hilgefort, Greenwich, CT; Peter Joseph, New York, NY; Bill & Donna Nussbaum, St. Louis, MO

Related Professional Experience: Workshop, Arrowmont School of Arts and Crafts, Gatlinburg, TN, 1992

Galleries: Brown/Grotta Gallery, Wilton, CT; Lick Log Mill Store, Highlands, NC

Publications: "Leon and Sharon Niehues," *The News Basket*, Vol. 4 No. 5, October 1987, pp. 22-25.; Niehues, Leon and Sharon Niehues, "Modern Traditional Basket," *The News Basket*, Vol. 4 No. 6, December 1987, pp. 12-14.

Sharon Niehues

(works with Leon Niehues)
Niehues Baskets
Rt 5 Box 305
Huntsville, Arkansas 72752

Born: Alton, Illinois, 1952

Awards/Honors: Fellowship, Arkansas Arts Council, 1992

Education: Lawrence High School, Kansas; Duncan High School, Duncan, Oklahoma; Tennessee Basketry Symposium with Michael Davis, 1987
    Self taught

Exhibitions: See Leon Niehues

Collections: See Leon Niehues

Galleries: See Leon Niehues

Publications: See Leon Niehues

Amy Pennebaker

(works with Ed Pennebaker)
Red Fern Glass
HC 68 Box 128
Green Forest, Arkansas 72638

Born: Akron, Ohio, 1958

Education: B.F.A. (enameling & textiles), Cleveland Institute of Art, Ohio

Galleries: The Edison Institute, Dearborn, MI; Smithsonian Institution Museum Shops, Washington, D.C.; Museum of American Folk Art, New York, NY; Sandwich Glass Museum, MA; Old Sturbridge Village, MA; Essex Institute, Salem, MA

Ed Pennebaker

(works with Amy Pennebaker)
Red Fern Glass
HC 68 Box 128
Green Forest, Arkansas 72638

Born: Pratt, Kansas, 1955

Education: M.A. (printmaking), Emporia State University, Kansas; B.F.A. (printmaking), Emporia State University, Kansas; A.A., Garden City Community College, Kansas; workshops with Sonja Blomdahl, Benjamin Moore

Related Professional Experience: Glassblower, Hale Farm and Village Glassworks, Bath, Ohio, 1983-1985

Galleries: See Amy Pennebaker

Helen Phillips

2801 N. Fillmore Street
Little Rock, Arkansas 72207

Born: Cincinnati, Ohio, 1938

Education: M.F.A. (ceramics), University of Florida; B.S. (art), Memphis State University, Tennessee; University of Hawaii, Manoa; Memphis Academy of Art, Tennessee

Exhibitions: 1993 - "New Ceramics," Creative Arts Workshop, New Haven, CT; "Clay and Fiber Exhibition," Octagon Center for the Arts, Ames, IA; "National Dishman Competition," Lamar University, Beaumont, TX; 1992 - "Brenau College National Invitational Art Exhibition," Gainesville, GA; " Mid-South Sculpture Invitational," University of Arkansas, Little Rock; "Eight Arkansas Women Artists," University of Arkansas, Fayetteville, "La Grange National XVIII," La Grange College, GA; "Currents '92," Middle Tennessee State University, Murfreesboro; "Form and Object: Contemporary Interpretations of Craft Traditions," University of Wyoming, Laramie; 1991 - "Works in Clay VII," Wichita Falls Museum and Art Center, TX; "Clay U.S.A., 1991," Radford University, VA; "Just Fired: New Ceramic Work," Tempe Arts Center, AZ; "34th Annual Delta Art Exhibition," The Arkansas Arts Center, Little Rock; "The Arkansas Collection: An Invitational," University of Arkansas at Little Rock; 1990 - "Wichita National," Wichita Art Association, KS; "Fifth Annual Monarch National Ceramic Competition," San Angelo Museum of Fine Arts, TX; "Regional Craft Biennial," The Arkansas Arts Center, Little Rock

Collections: Sanford M. and Diane Besser Collection, Little Rock; Ball State University, Muncie, IN; Allan Chasanoff, New York, NY; Orton Foundation of Ohio, Columbus; University of Arkansas at Little Rock Law School; University of Arkansas at Pine Bluff; University of Florida, Gainesville; The Arkansas Arts Center Foundation Collection, Little Rock

Related Professional Experience: Professor of art, University of Central Arkansas, Conway, 1976 - present; Adjunct instructor, University of Florida, 1975-76; adobe workshop at University of Texas at Tyler; The Arkansas Arts Center, Little Rock; Calabash Pottery, Fayetteville, AR

Laura Phillips

616 N. Cedar Street, Apt. 2
Little Rock, Arkansas 72205

Born: Memphis, Tennessee, 1958

Awards/Honors: Fellowship, Arkansas Arts Council, 1992

Education: M.F.A. (ceramics), Cranbrook Academy, Bloomfield Hills, Michigan; B.A., (art & Asian Studies), Connecticut College, New London; Doshisha University, Kyoto, Japan; Southeast Surface Design Workshop, Arrowmont School of Arts and Crafts, Gatlinburg, Tennessee; Omaha Brickworks Workshop with Jun Kaneko, Omaha, Nebraska; summer workshop, Alfred University, New York

Exhibitions: 1990 - "Faculty Exhibition," University of Arkansas at Little Rock; 1988 - "Regional Craft Biennial," The Arkansas Arts Center, Little Rock; 1987 - "28th Annual Delta Exhibition," The Arkansas Arts Center, Little Rock; solo exhibition, Honors Center Gallery, University of Central Arkansas, Conway; 1986 - "Connecticut College Alumni Show: Five Sculptors," Manwaring Gallery, New London; 1986 - "1st Annual Monarch Tile Ceramic Competition," San Angelo Museum of Fine Arts, TX

Collections: Arkansas Artists Registry, University of Arkansas at Little Rock; The Arkansas Arts Center Foundation Collection, Little Rock

Related Professional Experience: Instructor, The Arkansas Arts Center Museum School, Little Rock, 1985, 1988-1993; instructor, University of Arkansas at Little Rock, 1990; instructor of ceramics, University of Texas at Tyler, 1986; part-time instructor, University of Arkansas at Little Rock, 1985; instructor of ceramics, University of Central Arkansas, Conway, 1985

Galleries: Virginia Breier Gallery, San Francisco, CA; Maralyn Wilson Gallery, Birmingham, AL

Liz Powers

2522 Maybranch Drive
Fort Smith, Arkansas 72903

Born: Little Rock, Arkansas, 1941

Education: B.A., University of Arkansas, Fayetteville; The Sorbonne, Paris, France; Enameling course, The Arkansas Arts Center (Instructor B.J. Moses); Workshops at The Arkansas Arts Center with Colette and Arrowmont School of Arts and Crafts, Gatlinburg, Tennessee with Martha Banyas

Exhibitions: 1992 - Group exhibition, Arkansas Territorial Restoration, Little Rock

Collections: David & Pam Banks, Fort Smith, AR; Lucy Cabe, Little Rock; Ruth Remmel, Little Rock

Owen Rein

P.O. Box 1162
Mountain View, Arkansas 72560

Born: Ho Chi Minh City, Vietnam, 1956

Education: G.E.D; Bergen Community College, Paramus, New Jersey; Manhattanville College, Purchase, New York; Hoosack School of Design, North Adams, Massachusetts

Collections: Sara Spencer, Little Rock; Tom Hill, Memphis, TN

Related Professional Experience: Demonstrator, Ozark Folk Center, Mountain View, AR, 1988 - present

Publications - "Chair Maker" Vocational Biographies, Inc., Sauk Centre, MN, Series V, Vol. 7, No. 18, 1992.

Susy Siegele

(works with Michael Haley)
Buzzard Mountain Studios
Rt. 5 Box 775
Huntsville, Arkansas 72740

Born: Coffeyville, Kansas, 1953

Education: B.A. (art-ceramics), Texas Women's University - Denton; University of St. Thomas, Houston, Texas

Related Professional Experience: See Michael Haley

Galleries: See Michael Haley

Douglas Stowe

P.O. Box 247
Eureka Springs, Arkansas 72632

Born: Memphis, Tennessee, 1948

Education: B.A., (political science and sociology), Hastings College, Hastings, Nebraska; Memphis State University, Tennessee
    Self taught

Exhibitions: 1993 - "MOAK," Springfield, Art Museum, MO; "Lifestyles," Tokyo, Japan

Collections: Jim & Susan Nelson, Eureka Springs, AR

Related Profesional Experience: Workshops for Teche Woodworkers, New Iberia, LA

Mark Werner

HC 63, Box 476
Peel, Arkansas 72668

Born: New Hampton, Iowa, 1951

Awards/Honors: Fellowship, The Arkansas Arts Council, 1992; Fellowship, The Arkansas Arts Council, 1986

Education: B.F.A. (painting), Layton School of Art & Design, Milwaukee, Wisconsin; M.A. (painting), University of Iowa, Iowa City

Exhibitions: 1992 - "In/Form IV," St. Louis, MO; "35th Annual Delta Art Exhibition," The Arkansas Arts Center, Little Rock; "National Invitational," Brenau College, Gainesville, GA; 1988 - "31st Annual Delta Art Exhibition," The Arkansas Arts Center, Little Rock

Collections: Arkansas Arts Council, Little Rock; Baptist Medical Center, Little Rock; Devil's Den State Park, Winslow, AR; Grefe & Sidney Law Offices, Des Moines, IA; J.P. Hammerschmidt Plaza, Harrison, AR; Laura Musser Museum, Muscatine, IA; Lead Hill State Park, Diamond City, AR; Newsweek Magazine, Mountain Lakes, NJ; 125 Recreation Park, Peel, AR; Rose Law Firm, Little Rock; Traer Bank, IA; Toledo Bank, IA

Related Professional Experience: Workshops - "Introduction to Art," North Arkansas Community College, Harrison, AR, 1980; "Woodbine Art Fair" Woodbine, IA, 1976; Solo Artist Presentation, Halverson Center for Educational Research, Council Bluffs, IA, 1976; Artist in Residence, S. Tama High School, IA, 1974-75

Galleries: Claibourne Gallery, St. Louis, MO

The Arkansas Arts Center Board of Trustees

Officers

Curt F. Bradbury, Chairman

Phil L. Herrington, President

Harriet Stephens, Vice President

Hugh Randolph Wilbourn, Treasurer

George E. Campbell, Secretary

James H. Atkins
Pam Banks
Richard F. Bell
Ann Bemis
Sam Buchanan, Jr.
C. Douglas Buford, Jr.
Dr. Delbra Caradine
William E. Clark
Gayle Corley
Jack W. Forrest
Greer Grace
Pat Gray
H. Watt Gregory III
Dr. Ruth Herts
Mimi Hurst
Ben Hussman
Helene Meyer
Ark Monroe III
Donald Munro
Rosemarie Nunn
George R. O'Connor
A. Dan Phillips
Marilynn Porter
Betty Tucker
W. Jackson Williams

Ex-Officio Members

Jim Dailey, Mayor, City of Little Rock
Patrick Henry Hays, Mayor, City of North Little Rock
James T. Dyke, Chairman, The Arkansas Arts Center Foundation
Leslie Lee
Kay Spencer
Rita Vess

Honorary Members

Missy Anderson
Raida Pfeifer
Jeannette Edris Rockefeller, Chairman Emeritus

The Arkansas Arts Center Foundation Board of Directors

James T. Dyke, Chairman
Robert Shults, Vice Chairman
H.G. Frost, Jr., Treasurer
Townsend Wolfe, Secretary

Curt F. Bradbury
Ben Hussman
Howard Lutnick
H. Maurice Mitchell
Winthrop Paul Rockefeller
B. Finley Vinson

Phil L. Herrington, President
The Arkansas Arts Center Board of Trustees